I'm Not Forty

Female Edition

Jean Dawn Leigh

jadie
BOOKS

Published by
Jadie Books 2005

ISBN 0 9527082 5 6

Illustrations by Ian West

Typesetting by Jake Adie

Printed & bound by
Northstar Design
Colne
Lancs
BB8 9DB

Me Forty?

Oh God, how did I get myself into this mess? This is awful. Too awful for words. What am I going to have to do to get out of this one? Oh look, I'm so sorry, you haven't got a clue what I'm on about, have you? I do apologize, really. But listen, there's no harm in letting you in on my predicament. It could hardly make matters any worse. But you must promise to take me seriously. Please. Because, as you may have sensed, I'm having trouble seeing the lighter side of things at the moment. You see, my problem is I'm on the verge of not being forty. Yes, that's right, *not* forty. The big day is looming when I'm not going to be forty-years-old. The trouble is, I was thirty-nine this time last year so, you can imagine, everybody is going to expect me to automatically become forty. But I'm not going to. Honestly. Something rather strange seems to have occurred in my case and, unlike other normal people who take the event in their stride, I'm just not going to be able to make it. To be honest with you, I've suspected for some time now that something like this would happen to me and only wish that I'd prepared myself a bit better. You know, planned my approach more thoroughly. Could have made the whole thing a lot easier. But it's too late now and I've no choice but to face the music. Going to take some explaining though.

You understand that I'm not ready to be an FYO, don't you? I really don't resemble their type in any way. Never have done. They're so completely different to me that I'd look absurd if I even attempted to carry it off. For a start, they look nothing like me.

They dress differently, speak differently and have a sort of maturity that I couldn't even begin to copy. I mean, they're just older than me — they always have been. In fact, they've been around for almost as long as I can remember and I wouldn't be surprised if many of them weren't well into their fifties or even sixties by now. How can I possibly compete with that?

I know what's probably happened. There's been some kind of interstellar mathematical blip — you know, something totally beyond the control of us mere earthlings, and I've been caught in a sort of time warp. Well, something like that —

astrophysics isn't one of my strong points, I'm afraid. So, instead of just naturally passing from one age to another, I've ended up out of step with the rest of society and exist in some kind of chronological no-mans-land. How confusing. Maybe, if I'm lucky, things will just correct themselves without my needing to seek professional help. Could take some time I'll grant you, but I may get back on track within a couple of years or so. God, it's as though I've inherited some kind of growth disorder where the body develops at a different rate to other people's. Only mine's psychological rather than physical. Ehm, put like that it doesn't seem quite so bad. Gives me hope in a way. Maybe there's a course of drugs I could take to reset my neurological software. Could call in at the surgery on my way to work. No, on second thoughts, there's absolutely no way I'm going to even attempt to explain this to my GP. He's yet to recognize the existence of PMT. No chance he'd get his head around this one. I've simply got no choice. I'll just keep the whole damn business to myself and try to pretend that I'm no different to the next person. Well, what else can I do?

If I get working on a research programme to identify what it is that actually constitutes an FYO, there's no reason why I shouldn't be able to feign the whole thing. Just check out what they get up to, what their typical behavioural patterns are etc., and I should almost be there. Ehm, sounds okay to me. Right, what shall I take a look at first? How about their . . .

Clothes

As good a place as any I should think. So, what's different about the way they dress themselves? Any ideas? No problem. Just have to look frumpy. Shouldn't be difficult. Now, what's the best way to go about looking frumpy — you know, mummsie-like? Suppose I'll have to visit different types of shops.

God, this could be expensive — a whole new wardrobe? And I don't even want to look like them anyway. Perhaps I could buy a few sample outfits for when I'm with people who know me and, well, at other times dress as I do now. After all, it's unlikely that anybody's going to ask any questions. They're certainly not going to suspect anything, are they? Not with my youthful looks, surely? Yes, that's the answer and it'll be a far less costly business that way.

Okay, a plan of action. Start with the shoes, ehm, what sort do FYOs wear? Err, not so easy this. I know, Mum! She used to be an FYO. She's bound to have some of her old FYO shoes in the cupboard. I'll give her a ring. And she's probably got some of those funny clothes they wear as well. Now, jeans. I'll have to get some FYO denims for everyday use. They'll come in useful for a whole variety of occasions. Where do you buy them, I wonder? Hold on a minute, what's the difference between FYO jeans and normal ones? Is there one? Of course there is! Right, no need to part with any cash on that one. All I've got to do is fetch a couple of pairs of my own ones and press a permanent crease down the front and back of each leg. Mind you, it'll take some time to get that bleached stripe effect they all like on the crease. Wonder how they do it. Maybe I could just lay them out flat on the kitchen table and apply a diluted solution of bleach in a straight line with, err, yes, my cake icing kit. That should work. This is not turning out to be as difficult as I thought it might. Okay, what's next? Something that will look right with the jeans to complete the outfit. A jacket. The kind of jacket an FYO would choose. Sort of anoraky type of zip-up thing, I suppose. But, they're not really very much different to the ones I already wear. Peculiar. I'm sure they do look more sort of FYOish when I see them out. So what's the difference? Hold on, let me picture them in the high street for a second . . . yeah, right, done that. But they're the same as mine: nylon fabric, big pockets all over them, zips everywhere, colour doesn't seem too important. Ehm, I'm a bit stuck on this one. Let's take another look . . . try to picture it in my mind . . . Yes, it's coming, stay with me, yes, yes . . .GOT IT! Oh no, you wouldn't believe it. Really. No problem. All I've got to do is pop out and buy my better half an identical copy. That's all they do — walk around with matching jackets. Easy, eh?, that's if I can actually do it with a straight face.

Right, that's clothes sorted, what next? How about . . .

Is this going to be as easy? Let's think. What does an FYO do with her hair? More to the point, what do *I* do with my hair? Thank God you can't see it at the moment. Anyway, that's another story. I've somehow got to find a way of getting my hair to emulate an FYO's when I enter my impersonation mode. So, come on, try to get

your head round this one — what do they do with their hair? Come on girls, I need some help. You never know, it might happen to you one day. All right, I'll tell you; they don't have to do anything with it — it starts going grey all by itself. But how am I going to deal with that? Oh dear, I'm going to have to ask my stylist to put some grey highlights *in*. That's ridiculous. She spends the whole of her time carefully disguising them for her normal clientele and there's me asking for the very opposite. She'll think I've gone stark-raving-mad. Maybe I have. Maybe that's the trouble. Nothing to do with my age at all. Perhaps I'm just going a bit doolally. Well, so be it, little I can do about that now. Got to get used to the fact that I'll be spending a few pounds extra each month having the grey bits put in. But what am I to do at other times when I'm just being me? I have no intention of turning into a full-time FYO. No way. Don't even think about it. Hold on though. If FYOs have bits of grey appearing and then have the process reversed with the introduction of highlights, my new grey streaks are going to look out of place. It's going to be more difficult than I imagined. Friends who think I should have reached the BIG FOUR-O will, no doubt, expect to see the odd grey hairs appear and then disappear once I've been to the salon like any normal FYO. Which means that, in addition to having the grey highlights applied periodically, I'll have to return to the stylist in between times to have them disguised. Oh God, this is pathetic. What *is* my hairdresser going to think? She'll probably

have me committed to an asylum. And I'm not too sure I wouldn't disagree with her. No, there's only one thing for it — I'll need two separate hairdressers; one to apply the grey and one to apply the brown. That way, there'll at least be a chance that one of them will think I'm normal. What a palaver.
Better have a

quick look in the mirror to get an idea of exactly what I want. Ehm, a bit closer . . . oh my God where did they come from? They can't be. There's got to be something wrong with this mirror. Or, maybe it's a reflection of some kind. Yes, of course, a reflection from the curtains or something. Wow, for a minute I thought I was beginning to go grey myself. What a frightful thought.

Right, must move on. Where to next? Ehm, bit delicate but let's have a look at their attitude towards . . .

Sex

Oh dear, oh dear, I'm going to upset somebody now. Bit of a delicate subject, eh? Okay, let's get on with it. How about you and I agreeing, first of all, that we're rather partial to it, yes? All right, if you insist, we're pretty much addicted to it. That better? Well, it's nothing to be ashamed of, is it? Wasn't our choice to feel like

this. Just the way the Good Lord made us. I mean, if we weren't all born with the necessary self-replicating programme built in we wouldn't be here to tell the story anyway, would we? No, man's self-imposed social values have led us all to regard the inclination to reproduce as something we should feel guilty about. Well, for the record, I'd like you to know that I'm not at all comfortable with this perspective. Don't misunderstand me, in terms of fidelity, I'm the perfect model partner and, as far as my other half is aware, my oestrogen-producing cells have been working overtime since the day we met oblivious of the fact that any other males even exist in our society. And I have no intention of spoiling things for him after all these years. But, given that there is zero chance of him picking up a copy of this book, let alone opening it, it won't hurt for you and I to be a little more candid with each other where the subject of rampant, female lust is concerned. Agree? Right. Monogamy is a wonderful idea and, had God found time to put a little more work in during its early developmental stages, I do believe he could have pulled it off successfully. But sadly, due to his R and D department being either unrealistically optimistic where the matter of deadlines were concerned or simply under-funded, the concept finally reached production in a somewhat premature form and has since, unsurprisingly, failed to live up to its original ideals. However, several remnants of the basic theory continue, to this day, to provide society with a half-reasonable service by allowing both parties within a normal male/female relationship to successfully delude themselves into believing that each of them is the sole object of the other's attentions. And, quite remarkably, in most cases, the system functions in a fairly effective state of equilibrium with neither party managing, somehow, to grasp the fact that their opposite number continually harbours the selfsame passion for any number of members of the other sex as they themselves do. The ultimate definition of the concept of faith? Still, we shouldn't be too hard on Him; nobody's perfect and for all His

obvious
shortcomings, I
don't doubt that
He actually
meant well.
But what, I hear
you ask, does
this have to do
with FYOs? Well,
I'll tell you.
FYOs, by no
fault of their
own, reside at
the end of a long
line of
generations who
dedicated their
lives to the
notion that one
should resist the
urge to engage in

encounters of the sexual kind with whomever takes one's fancy and to even regard such activity with one's own partner as being dangerously close to the boundaries of vulgarity. The practice, of course, produced a highly volatile situation which, to cut a long story short, culminated in a certain German individual leading the way for communities throughout the world to commute their suppressed sexual desires into unbridled mass genocide. So, with all of their pent-up energy suitably expended and the process having turned a full circle, what do you think they did next? Yes, right first time; they duly returned home and bonked away to their hearts' content. As though there was no tomorrow. But as we know, old habits die hard and a generation of future FYOs followed with attitudes little different to those of their predecessors. Attitudes to which youngsters like you and I will never subscribe. No, I'd certainly know if I was a real

FYO, wouldn't I?
But you won't let
on to my other
half, will you?
Promise?
Besides, if I'm
going to stand
any chance of
pulling this
masquerading
off, I'll have to
keep pretty quiet
about my
proclivities in
this direction.
Anyway, let's get
on with our work
and examine
something else.
How about . . .

45

After all, everyone has friends, even FYOs. So it will be worth my spending a little time considering the sort of person who would most likely fit the bill in order that I may suitably avail myself to the individuals inclined to score highest in the FYO-street-cred stakes. Got to look as though I fit in properly on those inevitable

Friends

occasions when FYO networking is unavoidable. So, what sorts of friends do FYOs attract? Or, put another way, what sort of friends do FYOs make? We'll have to take a close look at what they might be inclined to value highly in their contemporaries. Something that gives them a general feeling of kinship, closeness. The kinds of characters with whom one may feel particularly comfortable and begin to develop an allegiance. Ehm, interesting. How will they differ from normal friends? One's for instance, that I would currently consider meet my own set of objectives? Not quite so easy, that. I mean, apart from the odd ex-school- or work-friend that I've, to some extent, managed to keep up with over the years, I don't really, well, no, come to think of it, there aren't many. Well, not *real* friends, anyway. Not ones you'd actually trust to unload your most private problems on to. They sort of disappeared when I decided to settle down and contribute to the world's growing population dilemma. Haven't really had a great deal of time for anything else since. But, of course, things are beginning to look a lot different lately. What with the youngsters becoming increasingly independent of me. So, I suppose that's it; FYOs find themselves at the stage where the distraction to whom they have devoted a large proportion of their adult lives wanders off casually with little more than a glance over the shoulder. And in the process, leaves them without friends and devoid of any real direction in life. Do you think this could happen to me? Hope not. Anyway, for the purpose of the exercise, I suppose I'll have to act as though it has and do precisely what they do: find some others in the same position. And then what? Well, proceed to feign friendship while taking care, along the way, not to let those with whom I have chosen to develop a rapport see that I am really at something of a

loose end.
Arrange regular
coffee mornings
and lunches in
trendy local wine
bars. Pretend I'm
totally at ease
with things the
way they are and
enthuse about
the splendid way
in which life is
unfolding for our
respective,
delightful
offspring. And to
ensure that I
come across
utterly
convincingly,
learn to perfect

the art of appearing genuinely interested in a new acquaintance's interminable catalogue of mid-life trials and tribulations while making sure I am wearing an outfit for which she would gladly donate her right upper limb. How will that do? Pitched about right? Yes, I thought so. No one will ever suss that I'm a sub-FYO in a month of Sundays. Nothing to it when you think about it. Must be almost there by now. Should be fairly well-equipped for most eventualities I would say. Although I haven't covered the subject FYO's . . .

Well, as FYOs do everything else differently there's no reason to suppose holidays will be an exception. Can't quite imagine how just yet but no doubt it will become glaringly obvious after a little thought. Must have been in close proximity to them on a number of occasions in all sorts of destinations so it

Holidays

shouldn't be too difficult to bring to mind their particular vacational inclinations. So, where should we look first? Location? No, they're all pretty general — cater for most tastes and age groups. Types of activities perhaps? No, once again, too wide a cross-section of individuals involved. Must be something special about FYOs' hols, but what? You certainly see plenty of them around the usual attractions: beaches, restaurants, amusement parks etc. Don't tell me I've finally found an area where I actually have something in common with people of that age. Surely not. No, wait a minute, I think I'm on to something. Ehm, there is a difference, of course there is. Been barking up the wrong tree. FYOs go to precisely the same locations as normal people. Enjoy the selfsame attractions as well and certainly wine and dine alongside the rest of us in all sorts of eating establishments. But there is a difference. A crucial difference. While ordinary holiday-makers are making the most of their time away from work or from whatever it is they've chosen to escape, our FYO friends are walking around with faces as long as the proverbial kites while being followed closely behind by two-point-four equally miserable-looking, shoe-gazing, adolescent teenagers. No, I know that number of offspring is an unlikely occurrence — it was supposed to comically represent the typical British family unit. Oh, never mind. Anyway, that is sadly what is in store for the vast majority of FYOs whose rapidly developing cherubs can't abide being seen in their parents' company, let alone spending fourteen days and nights under constant surveillance. The youngsters, naturally, think they're more than old enough to fly off somewhere with their mates but ma and pa know better. Well, they thought they did. Of course, all members of the party would have been immeasurably better off had they abandoned all ideas about the trip months beforehand. But, in the event, mum and dad were customarily struck down during the days leading up to the magic date with severe bouts of reality-absent optimism.

Always an unwise time for making plans. What a simply dreadful situation to find yourself in. Just imagine your own flesh and blood demonstrating in public their total contempt for the two very people who have all but sacrificed their lives for their well-being. Can you think of anything more depressing?

Thank God my kids are not like that. Believe me, they simply revel in every second they are able to spend in my company. But then they haven't got a traditional FYO mother, have they? Anyway the whole thing is purely academic this year because, would you believe it?, the two of them have both got important examinations at school and have suggested that it may be advantageous for them to skip coming away this year. They were, naturally, broken-hearted when they told us. Poor things. You can just imagine their disappointment can't you? But we duly consoled them by reminding them that there'll be another chance next year and that it would come round in no time at all. But, rather than cheer them, that only seemed to make matters worse. They just adore coming away with us. So, rather than rub salt in their wounds, we've chosen to abort all plans this year to ensure that we will be there for them. And in a way, that suits me fine. Gets me off the hook, so to speak. Could just arrange to go out for the odd day here and there. Maybe go to a concert even. Ehm, but what sort of concert? Have to be an FYO-style concert, I suppose. Must check out their tastes in . . .

Music

Well, I've always had fairly catholic tastes where the subject of music is concerned. Like almost anything really as long as it's performed well. Or, of course, if it has a particular significance to a time or place in our lives. Music's like that, isn't it? Sort of stirs things up inside you; takes you back years even and gets you all

weepy-eyed when you're least expecting it. But, then, it's different for us girls, don't you think? I mean, fellas approach the subject from a totally different perspective. To them, the artist actually performing the piece is of little consequence, of secondary importance in a way compared to the song itself.

They're strange like that. How can you ignore the very person responsible for interpreting the sentiments contained within the lyrics? It's the most relevant factor as far as us girls are concerned — any intelligent female will vouch for that. For instance, how could you possibly get all worked up and emotional while being serenaded by a short, pot-bellied, overweight, acne-faced individual rambling on about how tight he'd like to hold you? It just wouldn't work, would it? Not exactly the stuff fantasies are made of, eh? (All right, it's not what we tell our other halves but we all know that's about the measure of it.) If you didn't erase all knowledge of such a despicable character from your memory at the soonest opportunity you'd end up having nightmares. No, the songwriter's messenger has to be entirely credible if he wishes to sell himself to his female audiences. The song's lyrics are important but will always be secondary to the singer's hips, eh girls?

Right, that's that little matter sorted, now what kind of groove will I have to get into that will suit my aspirations to come across as a consummate FYO? More to the point, which performers will I need to target to avoid being seen at the wrong sort of venue? The type of venue full of young people like me. After all,

I can't afford to blow my cover over a simple thing like this. Have to see if any of those aging, born again, rock 'n roll singers with upper-lip afflictions are due to do any British dates this year. Be able to queue up with their back-combed-hair-styled, white ankle-socked, middle-aged followers desperate to catch a glimpse of their idol. Might even manage a scream or two when he attempts one of his embarrassing replacement hip-wiggles. Know the kind of thing? Strange though because these guys don't look an awful lot different to the way they did in the old days, do they? Must have found the elusive elixir. But if you take a look at their followers . . . well, there's not quite such a resemblance, is there? Haven't somehow weathered the years quite so well as their idols and I reckon that's the attraction, don't you? Watching them cavort about on stage like teenagers must delude those in the audience into believing they're a couple of decades younger themselves. Have to go along with it all I suppose. God, is this going to be dull or what? Do people actually enjoy being forty?

Be good practice though just in case I ever end up being an FYO myself. Must have covered everything by now. All ready to get out there and give it a go. No

one will know
the difference I'm
sure. Hold on,
I've forgotten
something; what
do they do to fill
their spare time?
No reason to
think FYOs don't
have spare time
on their hands
like the rest of
us, is there?
Better take a
look at their . . .

Music

The sorts of things they do with whatever physical abilities they have left at their disposal. Not many I should imagine. Which will narrow the field down a touch and, in the process, make it easier to pretend I'm enjoying myself. Now, let me see, we must have a choice here. Nothing too strenuous of course. Right,

Hobbies

how about flower arranging? Or, maybe, collecting something like stamps or odd-shaped wine bottles — ehm, wine bottles, a bit more culturally significant, don't you think? Yes, *bouteilles à vin* it will be. No, hold on, not wine bottles, no, the stuff they put inside them: wine! That sounds more like it. I'll become a wine connoisseur. Be able to impress people as one of them. Give talks to local societies. Might even enjoy this one. Have to take it seriously, mind you. Can't put myself about as a self-confessed wine buff if I don't know my *rouge* from my *blanc*. Although, of course, I'll be in good company because wine-snobbery is, as we all know, one of the fundamental differences between FYOs and youngsters like me. I'll be able to play them at their own game. Should be fun. Be able to do that thing in restaurants when the wine waiter offers to let you taste a sample before he commits the whole table to it. You know, when you have to swirl the stuff around in the glass before poking your nose in and inhaling deeply with an ever-so-serious expression on your face. And then, the really professional bit, when you sit mummified for about half-a-minute with a quizzical look on your face while your not-so-expert friends wait anxiously for your verdict.

This is the real convincing bit, the bit that makes playing the snob role all the more worthwhile. For one frozen moment in time they sit rigidly watching your every movement eager to learn what they will be allowed to put to their lips. It's all that matters in the world to them. What responsibility. What sheer power. Total control of what they should use to wash their ensuing meal down with. Only you are qualified to be trusted with matters of such orders of magnitude. No one else. Your standing in society will increase fourfold overnight. And all because you know something they don't. Not the quality of the wine. Or its compatibility with the meal about to be consumed. Of course not. No, you see, you enjoy exclusive access to *their* taste buds. More so, in fact, than they do themselves. You will be blessed with the curious ability to know what will give *them* pleasure. Not just you, *them*. Amazing or what? I mean, who's kidding who? What is it with these FYOs? How, if you'll excuse the pun, can they seriously swallow such utter codswallop? Well, they wouldn't apply the principle to any other subject, would they? Like, "Here, Susie, would you mind listening to this new CD to see if I'd like it?" or, "Be a darling Sarah and take

this chap home
with you for a
couple of nights
— like to know if
he'd be able to
satisfy me." I tell
you, FYOs and
wine are the first
steps towards
senility.
Honestly. Makes
no sense
whatsoever.
Sure, I'll go
through with it
just to make the
real FYOs in my
company feel a
little more
comfortable but
when I find

myself alone or when I'm mixing with youngsters of my own age I'll jolly well stick to the port. A proper drink with plenty of real body to it. Not just any old port, mind you. No, it has to be a decent vintage. And not any old vintage year at that. Oh no, you won't catch me out there. Got to be the real thing. You see, I know all about port. I know instinctively whether it's worth drinking just by glancing at the bottle. Important judgements of that kind need to be left to experts like me. Not just any old after dinner drinker. In fact, maybe that's the answer to all my problems — a couple of bottles of the old red stuff and this whole FYO business won't matter in the slightest. Yes, I reckon that's the answer.